MW00781655

BALANCE
IS A JUGGLING ACT

*How to Start a Mental Revolution
for a Change in Thought*

RAIYSA DARLENE
NAZAIRE

ISBN (Print): 978-1-09838-045-8
ISBN (eBook): 978-1-09838-046-5

This work is dedicated to each one of us
as we strive to ascertain personal and communal balance
in uncertain times by regaining control of something
that is uniquely ours—our thoughts.

We can enhance our lives one thought at a time,
from there we enhance the world.

Raiysa Nazaire

Download *Your Balance Toolkit* Free!

*J*ust to say thank you for buying my book, I would like to give you the companion ***Your Balance Toolkit*** free!

This guide will help you to identify the well-being tools that will work best for you to live a life of high-potential energy that propels you to complete your life's mission. I describe the major tools and their purpose. It is up to you to experiment to find the right set up tools to complete your personal balance toolkit.

TO DOWNLOAD GO TO
https://designrr.page/?id=93884&token=2501024811&type=FP

Contents

Phase 3: Self-Encounter

Phase 4: Conscious Living

Foreword

My journey into mental well-being started with trauma. The reason I became so fascinated with helping people understand mental health as a means to experience a better quality of life and joy is my son Khaliyq, who died by suicide in 2008 from what was labeled as undiagnosed depression. I wondered how someone who was so full of vigor and promise could fall into imbalance so severe that the best solution his mind could think of was to take his life to end the mental pain. So, I started to study mental health. I found that Khaliyq was a near text-book study for mental distress. I felt robbed that information on mental distress was not more readily available. I wanted everyone to know that mental distress is treatable and preventable. In fact, my own mental balance as a mother who lost her son to suicide depended upon my learning of true mental health. I had watched what falling into despair due to the death of a child did. I had also witnessed the extreme impact of repression of these emotions. I chose not to go down either of those rabbit holes. Neither honored the brilliance of my son, nor the fact that I still had a life to love. So, I decided to become a mental health advocate.

The more I learned, the more I realized that mental distress need not be the epidemic that it is. A simple education in mental well-being can help everyone live a more fulfilling and joyful life. My study led to the formation of a not-for-profit organization for suicide awareness and prevention–The Young Tiger Foundation (after the Morehouse Tigers), a book about my son's life called *Leaping Over the Hurdles of Life,* a personal conscious mental balance practice, and this book. This work demonstrates how mental balance is an everyday life practice for your life. I aim to make this knowledge go viral.

Introduction

Thoughts are produced from our mental being, our mind. Thoughts determine what actions we take, how we express ourselves, and how we interact with others. The quality and clarity of our thoughts is dependent upon our mental state. Strangely, the topic of mental health is a societal taboo. It is generally not taught at home, or in school, nor is it a topic addressed on most annual physical exams. As a society, we do not acknowledge or value mental health as our true source of wealth. So it is no wonder that, when something so fundamental to making healthier decisions that support rational, organized thought processes, and balanced emotions and actions is left out, we have so much instability in the world.

The following is what I have found to be true.

- The human emotional default state of being is compassion and love.

- Mental balance is the foundation of a life well lived.

- Balanced people do not spread fear, division or hate.

- Mental balance is the answer to societal ills.

Balance, however, is not a steady state. It must be managed. Like juggling balls in the air, it can be difficult to keep healthy, balanced thoughts flowing effortlessly. Like juggling, once you grasp and get the rhythm of key mental well-being concepts, mental balance becomes a skill that you can master.

This book is a guide on how to start a mental revolution for a change of thought, with the goal of enhancing your life one thought at a time. The change that starts with you will morph into a mental health revolution for a new way of being that can ultimately ripple into a balanced world.

Good mental health has the power to transform and energize your life experience because it boosts your mood, thinking and behavior.

The average person has no knowledge of what mental health is. This lack of knowledge makes life much harder and less joyful than it need be. Therefore, a mental revolution for a change in thought is needed.

To set this revolution and mind expansion into play, I ask you to give mental well-being your focus for forty days, using this book as an entry point to board your personal Noah's ark from world chaos, to emerge from a mental storm as a more balanced and fulfilled being. You will be amazed at the shift in your energy and the outward results in your life.

To begin this journey from as grounded a state as possible, here is the World Health Organization's definition of mental health:

"a state of well-being in which every individual realizes his or her own potential, can cope with the normal stresses of life, can work productively and fruitfully, and is able to make a contribution to her or his community."

This is a great definition, especially when we unpack it further. It suggests that mentally balanced people embody the following characteristics.

1. They are comfortable being their authentic selves. They do not conform for the sake of fitting into limiting societal norms. Each of

us can tap into our personal strengths and express these gifts in our unique ways.

2. Their ability to cope is stronger than life's stressors. In this definition, life's stressors are handled with balance. We are not diminished by fear and we can adapt to newly normal situations.

3. They remain productive and fruitful despite the environment. Balanced people have the flexibility to learn new skills and adapt to change. There is a flow to their lives through which dreams and goals are accomplished with grace.

4. They have a sense of purpose. Balanced individuals are cognizant that we are on this planet to help one another. The way we help each other is by bringing our unique puzzle pieces and laying them upon the table of unity.

When you have true mental balance, you are aware that you are an integral part of the greater whole. It is important to recognize how this crazy (and amazing) world is affected by every one of us.

As abnormal stressors come (such as the global pandemic's tolls on life, fixed institutions, and economics), you can respond productively and fruit-fully, and you continue to make contributions to yourself and your community. This means using mental well-being to stay deeply rooted in balance by swaying like a healthy deeply rooted tree during a storm. We are being called to shift, reflect, re-frame, and re-prioritize. Being incredibly open to learning and adapting will be the difference between thriving and simply surviving. We will create viable solutions for personal and societal challenges. We have that power.

Since change is inevitable, balance and self-mastery are essential to maintaining well-being and living a life of joy. Mental balance and self-mastery have similar attributes. They are both:

- a state of awareness or clarity in the moment,

- a state of being that gives you freedom to move spontaneously,

- the ability to respond to what is needed in the moment with the appropriate action (or inaction),

- dynamic and subject to upgrades as we learn more, and

- manifested in the state of being present.

Poor mental balance is epidemic. At this writing, one in five people worldwide are experiencing significant imbalance. This imbalance shows up in many ways: from the anxiety prompted by unstable leadership, and the constant—and instant—access to information, to the feelings of isolation and a suddenly uncertain future.

Poor mental health also appears in our conditioning, forcing us to keep recycling the limited thoughts that stop us from living the life that we desire. Since our thoughts and emotions are the basis of mental health, and thoughts and emotions create our life experience, why is there a stigma around mental health? Is it simply the fear of poor mental health? I invite you to ditch the stigma and embrace the empowerment that comes with focused mental well-being.

You can use this book to learn more about improving your own quality of life, in addition to supporting and having compassion for others who may be struggling.

Mental health or balance requires self-observation and flexible adjustment. This juggling act of continual motion teaches you to navigate life's challenges with greater confidence and ease.

How to Get the Most Out of This Book

Each day you will review a foundational concept of mental balance. The objective is to engage in the transformative process of expanding your mind by shifting your perspective through recording your morning thoughts, your daily exploration, and your evening reflection.

1. Morning Thoughts: after a morning reading of the concept of the day, jot down your thoughts on the mental well-being concept, then

2. Daily Exploration: see where the concept shows up during the day. Just noticing is a step toward making empowered change.

3. Evening Reflection and Awareness Gained: use this second notation to explore how the concept was able to be used throughout the day (capturing any thoughts or aha moments experienced) or acknowledging when you caught a thought before it spiraled into fear or self-limitation. Do this prior to going to bed.

The book is divided into four sections, and each contains ten mental well-being concepts followed by a mental-balancing exercise called a "balancing act." They are:

Awareness - becoming more aware of what is going on in the background of your thought process and automatic behaviors,

Self-Observation - watching how your thoughts lead to emotions and play out in your life,

Self-Encounter - learning more about how the mind and brain interact and adjusting learned patterns for balance, and

Conscious Living - incorporating the practice of conscious awareness in your daily life for overall well-being.

For forty days embrace being a Mental Balance Revolutionary—a proponent for a more balanced self and world. This approach to life is revolutionary because the average person spends no daily time dedicated to their mental well-being and no budget is set for mental health enrichment. This attention is needed to push through perceived mental limits to awaken unlimited personal potential. The ability to do so lies in our capacity to tap into higher-potential thoughts.

Have fun with this. On the next page is the first opportunity to "Expand your mind."

Expand your mind

Previously, what came to mind when you thought about mental health?
How could a shift in perspective, based on this introduction,
change the way you approach life?

_____

_____

_____

_____

_____

_____

_____

_____

_____

_____

_____

_____

_____

PHASE 1

AWARENESS

THOUGHTS ARE LIKE PASSING TRAINS. ONLY BOARD THOSE THAT TAKE YOU IN THE DIRECTION YOU WANT TO TRAVEL.

DAY 1
All Thoughts Are Not Created Equally!

Thoughts are fleeting. A thought is simply a momentary assessment that reflects your current state of mental balance as it is informed by past life experience.

You live in an overstimulating world designed to influence your thinking and subsequent behavior. Once you recognize that, you can begin a filtration process to remove lower-potential thoughts—the ones that do not lead you in the direction of your desire. The first filter removes the thoughts that are not yours, the second removes thoughts that are obsolete or untrue, and the third pushes to the forefront useful or higher-potential thoughts that you can use to move forward in life.

Ask yourself: Why do I believe this thought? Does having this thought help me get my desired results?

Treat thoughts like trains pulling into a station—only board them if they have the potential to take you in the direction of your desire. Where do you want to go? First, decide.

The prefix *de* in the word *decide* means *off* or *from*. The suffix *cide* means *to kill*. Decide means to kill off. It shares the same suffix as homicide or suicide. When you truly decide, you kill off a myriad of undesired possibilities and focus on achieving an act or goal, in whatever form you desire. Quantum physics tells us that focused, energized thought makes undesired possibilities less likely to occur.

Today, begin to take control of your well-being by evaluating your thoughts. Decide not to give energy to lower-potential thoughts. This is the first step towards balanced mental well-being.

Expand your mind

Morning Thoughts

_____

_____

_____

_____

_____

_____

Evening Summary and Insight Gained

_____

_____

_____

_____

_____

_____

DAY 2

Change Your Thoughts, Change Your Perspective, Change Your Life

Changing your thoughts from conditioned to open-minded shifts what appears for you. It gets you out of your current life path, opens new possibilities, and moves you to a new, as-yet unknown road. The unknown, viewed without fear, is a vast field of potential from which all things emerge and evolve. However, human default is to avoid the unknown in a desire to have control, which limits life to cycles of the same experiences—different day, variations of the same situations. Stepping into the unknown releases you from this endless loop.

Thoughts snowball in momentum to propel you in the direction of what you already believe and think. This is how worry becomes anxiety and anxiety escalates to severe anxiety or paranoia. A thought in motion does not stop until it encounters a more energized thought that displaces it. For example, anxious thoughts around giving a speech are diminished by thoughts of knowing you are prepared and that you share helpful information.

This awareness gives you the impetus to catch thoughts early on to ask how they serve you, instead of you habitually serving them. You take the time to:

- recognize lower-potential thoughts,
- search for the root cause of these thoughts,
- see if they are true now, and
- reframe thoughts using a clearer perspective.

This is active mental balance.

Today, look at the picture you are painting picture of life. How do you like it? Be flexible to see where you might adjust your perspective.

Expand your mind

Morning Thoughts

_____

_____

_____

_____

_____

_____

Evening Summary and Insight Gained

_____

_____

_____

_____

_____

_____

DAY 3
Thoughts Either Generate Flowers or Weeds

Untended weeds take over a garden. In a similar manner, unfocused thoughts take over your mind and your life.

Weeds adapt quickly to any environment. They grow strong and fast, sucking up vital nutrients before your fruitful flowers can get them. Unfocused thoughts behave the same way: they rob you of the energy and momentum needed to transform budding creative thoughts into flowers of reality.

Even when you pluck weeds to cultivate an environment where they are not welcome, they will continue to pop up. If you have meditated, you know how persistent weed-like thoughts can be. Your challenge is to allow weed-like thoughts to recede to the background of your consciousness.

Some weeds hide under other plants. That is similar to the way in which subconscious thoughts trigger undesirable actions.

The hardest weeds to get rid of are the ones that disguise themselves as the fruitful flower being cultivated. These imposters look like the real thing, just as subliminally induced and inherited thoughts from family or society present themselves as your own. Only examination will tell you the difference between the weed and the fruitful flower.

Be intentional about the seeds of thought you plant. You determine whether they will grow into weeds or fruitful flowers.

Today, observe your thoughts to see if you can find the weed-like thoughts that rob you of energy and momentum.

Expand your mind

Morning Thoughts

_____

_____

_____

_____

_____

_____

Evening Summary and Insight Gained

_____

_____

_____

_____

_____

_____

DAY 4

Obsolete Thoughts and Beliefs Ransom Your Future

To the body, acting on old thoughts, actions, and patterns is equivalent to reliving a past experience. The brain has already written a program for the response and immediately knows what to do. It jumps into action (re-acts). Yet, while the reaction may feel known and safe, it may not be the most appropriate response in the here and now. You will be able to discern the difference because reactions limit your ability to move forward in life.

For example, you want to learn to swim well; yet you feel that you cannot because of a fear of drowning. That fear may be rooted in a near-drowning experience as a child. Do you see how past fear can stifle future desire?

When you value your future more than holding on to the past, fear diminishes, progression occurs, and happiness increases. Like a rocket journeying into space, as you release that which weighs you down, you can soar higher; what was previously impossible becomes possible.

You learn that fear comes from your thoughts, not what is happening now or what is possible in this moment. With practice, you will be able to blast past the confines of your limiting beliefs and a subconscious false sense of comfort.

Today, as limiting beliefs come up, question them and write down what type of beliefs you would like to use to replace them. See what happens when future actions are taken from this new state of authority.

Expand your mind

Morning Thoughts

_____

_____

_____

_____

_____

_____

Evening Summary and Insight Gained

_____

_____

_____

_____

_____

_____

DAY 5

The First Place to Make Safe Is Your Mind

We have been taught to put more emphasis on physical health than mental health.

There is no doubt that they are both important, yet strong mental health will allow for a better experience when you are dealing with poor physical health. Strong mental health will also provide the inspiration to take better care of your body. Therefore, the first place to make safe is your mind.

The basic steps to support mental and physical health are similar.

- Drink sufficient clean water.
- Eat a well-balanced diet.
- Boost your immune system
- Get routine check-ups and tests.
- Incorporate regular exercise into your schedule.

The specifics differ. For example, you can use conscious awareness to boost your mental immune system to ward off *thought viruses*. A thought virus is an idea or concept that is passed on to you that is accepted without questioning its origin and/or validity. You take in a belief without knowing why it is accepted. Thought viruses take over the mind, and rational thinking is abandoned. Generational racism is an example of a thought virus.

The mind is also made safe by ceasing resistance to the unwanted. Ultimately, if you can relax to feel safe in your mind, body, and spirit, with a sense of "I am okay," you will relax to allow your highest potential to flow to you.

Today, build a plan for how you will make your mind safe from a holistic point of view.

Expand your mind

Morning Thoughts

_____

_____

_____

_____

_____

_____

_____

Evening Summary and Insight Gained

_____

_____

_____

_____

_____

_____

_____

DAY 6
Be Kind to Your Mind

Ideally, a mind dwelling in the present moment receives intuitive knowledge. Yet most of the time, the mind is anchored in the past, running on old programming to protect the self from the recurrence of past trauma. In protection mode, the mind does not take the time to scan the environment to see if a scenario still holds true.

The brain has created a shortcut, called a neural network, that responds to specific stimuli as they appear. Over time, this bundled message unit develops a habitual response in which the active brain is bypassed and the body's auto-response system takes over. This is the backward process of the body running the mind, instead of the mind running the body.

Speak kindly to your mind. Remind it that its job is to receive energized thought to direct the amazing instrument that is the body in having rewarding life experiences.

Today, observe to see if your mind is dwelling in the past based on your thoughts and actions. Gently nudge it toward the present moment.

Expand your mind

Morning Thoughts

_____

_____

_____

_____

_____

_____

Evening Summary and Insight Gained

_____

_____

_____

_____

_____

_____

_____

DAY 7
Maintaining Balance Requires Moment-to-Moment Commitment

Your mind is your entry point to the world. Everything that you experience is a function of your state of mind. With the goal to stay as centered as possible, compare emotional states to a pendulum that swings back and forth. The closer that pendulum is to the center, the more balanced you are.

The outer limits represent emotional highs or lows. Before you swing out too far, you can identify how you are feeling without judgement, name the feeling, and use time to balance. Then later, when calm, explore how to resolve any issue.

A balanced state of mind allows you to reign in your feelings while still acknowledging them. Managing the mental state you live in (called mind management) is simply a matter of practice.

Turning inward is critical to hearing your inner self, your well-being and your uniqueness.

Today, take mini timeouts to hear your own thoughts and find balance.

Expand your mind

Morning Thoughts

_____

_____

_____

_____

_____

_____

_____

Evening Summary and Insight Gained

_____

_____

_____

_____

_____

_____

_____

DAY 8

Know What State You Are in At All Times

I am not referring to your physical state. Know your state of mind. In any challenging situation, ask yourself, *Am I responding from a balanced state?* If you do not consciously know where your mind is, your breath will tell you. Is your breathing slow and relaxed, fast and shallow, or are you holding your breath? As you enter fight, flight or freeze mode, the breath shortens.

Have you noticed that during stressful situations it is a natural reaction to hold your breath? This hold locks in place the tension of a difficult moment. You send a message to the brain that you are distressed. As you repeat this action over time, you habitually breathe less fully. As a result, oxygen flow throughout your cells is diminished. The result is less energy and decreased vibrancy.

The shortest route to returning to balance is through the breath. Breath work allows space for something deeper than thought, conscious awareness, to come to the forefront.

Today, check in to see what mental state you are in, and use time to fully breathe and return your mind and body to homeostasis as needed. Feel the aliveness.

Expand your mind

Morning Thoughts

_____

_____

_____

_____

_____

_____

Evening Summary and Insight Gained

_____

_____

_____

_____

_____

_____

DAY 9

See Emotions as Indicators, Not Dictators

Acknowledging your feelings and emotions while allowing time to move through them is another cornerstone of mental well-being.

Every emotion, as energy in motion, has a message for you. For example, fear tells you that you are being threatened. Something immediate needs to be done to remove yourself from danger. When you use the energy of fear to drive you towards solutions to remove or lessen the threat, fear dissipates accordingly.

Emotions follow the focus of your thoughts and are precursors to the range of experiences you will face based on your thoughts. So, if you are sad and focus on sad thoughts, sad things and experiences will be magnified in your world. This does not mean you should ignore the reason for the sadness. It means that you move through a lower-potential emotion, such as sadness, without getting stuck in it.

Can you look at emotions as data for consideration? If so, they can used to bring about higher-potential outcomes.

We are human, so we are going to react. Reaction comes from the brain jumping into protection mode to send instructions to the body, pulled from its database of experience, to ensure survival. The data base of experience is driven by beliefs and prejudices that come from the unconscious mind. Yet, the current situation is never the same as past experience.

The unconscious mind prompts us to do things without thinking. This is good for a life-or-death situation, yet it is not so helpful with normal daily interaction. When we add the layer of reaction informed by observation of the current scenario and its impact on others, reaction is turned into response. Response is the ability to act appropriately. It draws information from both the conscious and unconscious mind. Responding allows us to think and act with higher potential than an emotion would dictate.

Today, when you see yourself applying a knee-jerk reaction based on an emotion, see if you can slow down to give yourself the opportunity to respond instead. Notice the empowerment in response.

Expand your mind

Morning Thoughts

_____

_____

_____

_____

_____

_____

Evening Summary and Insight Gained

_____

_____

_____

_____

_____

_____

_____

The Emotional Guidance Scale of High and Low Potential Emotions

Life experience is determined by our state of mind. At any moment in time our state of mind lies at some point on the spectrum of The Emotional Guidance Scale.

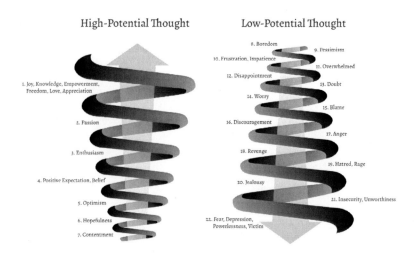

High-Potential Thought

1. Joy, Knowledge, Empowerment, Freedom, Love, Appreciation
2. Passion
3. Enthusiasm
4. Positive Expectation, Belief
5. Optimism
6. Hopefulness
7. Contentment

Low-Potential Thought

8. Boredom
9. Pessimism
10. Frustration, Impatience
11. Overwhelmed
12. Disappointment
13. Doubt
14. Worry
15. Blame
16. Discouragement
17. Anger
18. Revenge
19. Hatred, Rage
20. Jealousy
21. Insecurity, Unworthiness
22. Fear, Depression, Powerlessness, Victim

*The Emotional Guidance Scale is by Abraham-Hicks, © by Jerry & Esther Hicks, from "Ask & It is Given", AbrahamHicks.com website, contact (830) 755-2299

As we practice mental balance, we learn to shift to higher-potential emotions.

DAY 10

Emotions Are Frequencies that Attract Like Frequencies

Our society focuses on neither well-being nor on curing imbalance. Rather, it highlights distress via the news, and offers temporary bandages for all forms of imbalance. The commercial pharmaceutical industry is a good example of this practice.

It takes concentrated focus to maintain a forward-looking outlook. The key to maintaining this healthy perspective is holding the expectation of well-being and aligning with a higher emotion than the one being experienced.

The emotions on the Emotional Guidance Scale are ones we have all experienced to some degree or another. Emotions are frequencies, or energy in motion. Each emotion has a range of potential from which to create life experience. For example, you cannot experience appreciation while experiencing the emotion or frequency of jealousy. The associated emotional state of jealousy is craving from a sense of lack. Life from that viewpoint or frequency shows up as experiences dictated by insecurity and disappointment.

When experiencing a lower emotion, look around the bend and expect to spiral up to higher and higher points on the emotional scale of well-being. You may not be able to leap from the contractive emotion of depression to an expansive emotion of joy, yet happiness is just around the bend on the emotional scale of balance.

Sometimes growth feels like imbalance. Still, even moving from anger to discouragement is an energetic improvement. Understanding mental health lets you know that as you shift it is okay (and natural) to feel your way through awkward stages and uncomfortable emotions.

Today, practice shifting from a lower-potential emotion on the scale to a higher-potential one. Hint, gratitude for what you already have is one way to spiral up. Gratitude is the emotional gift that keeps on giving.

Expand your mind

Morning Thoughts

_____

_____

_____

_____

_____

_____

Evening Summary and Insight Gained

_____

_____

_____

_____

_____

_____

_____

Balancing Act –
THOUGHT OBSERVATION

Generally, the object of meditation is to quiet your thoughts. The object of today's Balancing Act is to sit quietly with your eyes closed for ten minutes and listen to the thoughts that pass through your mind.

Notice:

- which thoughts jump out first,

- which ones reoccur,

- which ones take you down a path spiraling away from the balancing act exercise, and

- any limiting themes that put a ceiling on your happiness.

Just notice with curiosity.

When I do this exercise, it gives me a clear understanding of what is troubling me and of any fearful themes that are being recycled in my mind. Giving these thoughts the opportunity to come up allows me to acknowledge them and let them know they have been heard. I then decide which thoughts to move forward with from that space of conscious awareness.

PHASE 2

SELF

OBSERVATION

EXAMINE YOUR THOUGHTS. ARE THEY DETRACTORS OR ADVOCATORS?

The Oscillation of Brain Waves

Each brain wave, or frequency, has a purpose that influences well-being. You are constantly shifting brain frequencies in response to what you are thinking about what is going on in your environment.

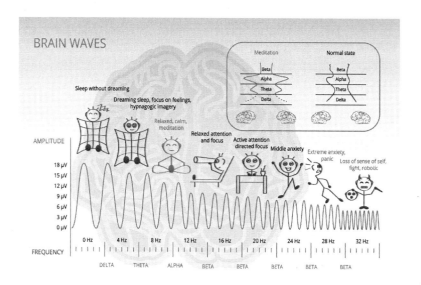

When you learn to align with the frequency that best serves your current purpose life experience is greatly enhanced. This knowledge will help you as you move through Phase 2, Self-Observation.

DAY 11
Actively Shift Brain Frequencies as Needed for Balance

As you can see from the brain-frequency image, the key to mental well-being lies in your frequency. As you move throughout a twenty-four-hour day, you may experience the brain firing from delta to high beta frequencies or brain waves.

While actively learning, you want to be in the beta frequency for active attention and focus. To the extreme, high beta represents a state of restlessness. In this frequency you experience a lot of mental noise and it uses a lot of mental energy. The voice in your head dominates and it is easy to become trapped by thoughts. For relief, you can shift to a brain frequency deeper than thinking. When tapping into higher states of consciousness during meditation or sleep, you move to lower frequencies of alpha (relaxed, focused attention in the present), theta (creativity, intuition), and delta (restorative sleep). Alpha is the brain's resting state.

Theta is characterized by long, deep breaths, versus high beta on the other end of the spectrum being characterized by short, shallow breaths. Since brain frequency follows the breath, you can use conscious deep breathing to shift brain frequencies. Binaural beats also facilitate this process.

The slower the brain wave—measured in hertz (the number of cycles per second of a brain wave)—the higher the frequency or energy. Frequencies also align to feelings and emotions.

Gamma (not shown on the chart) is the highest frequency yet it has the shortest wavelength. Its high frequency provides a burst of energy that yields instant revelation, knowing, and aha moments.

You are learning a new way of approaching balancing your energy. Today, as you go through daily activities, observe what brain frequency you are in based on how you are feeling.

Expand your mind

Morning Thoughts

_____

_____

_____

_____

_____

_____

_____

Evening Summary and Insight Gained

_____

_____

_____

_____

_____

_____

_____

DAY 12
Please Do Not Feed the Fears

Feeding fear, like feeding the bears, can land you in trouble. Fear relies on you for survival. Like adding logs to a fire to keep the blaze going, you have to keep generating fearful thoughts in order to sustain the emotion of fear (or any other emotion). The more fearful thoughts you have, the more fear escalates. Hesitation, procrastination, self-criticism, and doubt all feed fear. Constantly listening to news programs also stokes and escalates fear.

You can deescalate the situation by acknowledging the following:

1. Fear is your inner alarm system. Thankfully, it tells you that action is required to deal with potentially harmful stimulus in your environment. Yet, much like an alarm that goes off at the wrong time or stays on too long, prolonged fear eventually causes distress.

2. If you do not manage your fears, fear will determine what you can have and experience in life. All the fearful and low-potential what-if scenarios that run through your brain can easily be replaced with high-potential scenarios. Focus on high-potential what ifs.

3. Rather than jumping from a fearful thought to a fearful emotion that results in fearful action, feel the fear and listen for its message. Knowledge is the antidote to fear. Once the balancing action is realized, fear is released because there is nothing left to fuel it.

The practice of ceasing to feed fear helps you maintain power and energy. The mental adjustments made to cope and move forward—rather than stay stuck in emotions—determine the degree of equanimity that can be experienced in even the most traumatic situations.

Today, when the fear alarm goes off, find the message that fear is sharing, then proceed responsibly.

Expand your mind

Morning Thoughts

_____

_____

_____

_____

_____

_____

Evening Summary and Insight Gained

_____

_____

_____

_____

_____

_____

_____

DAY 13
Know Your Personal Kryptonite

Your personal kryptonite is the person, place, or thing that drains your energy mentally, emotionally, physically, or spiritually. Kryptonite is the thing that falsely triggers neural networks in your brain to send you into fight, flight, or freeze.

Are you cognizant of who or what triggers your sense of balance?

This may be a person who leaves you feeling sick or weak after spending time with them. It may be a place that makes you feel sad. Or it may be an object that enrages you for some buried reason.

Learning to avoid or mitigate triggers, until they no longer hold power, helps you stay emotionally strong.

Knowing yourself and what causes you to be unhappy and unfulfilled is key to personal balance and well-being.

Today, use time to acknowledge what triggers you, and plan how you will avoid being so forcefully impacted during the next encounter. Note that this will likely take repeated practice.

Expand your mind

Morning Thoughts

_____

_____

_____

_____

_____

_____

_____

Evening Summary and Insight Gained

_____

_____

_____

_____

_____

_____

_____

DAY 14
Learn to Manage Your Emotional Calendar

We all have an emotional calendar. Its history begins in your genes. Day one starts in the womb and you add new holidays and celebrate anniversaries throughout life. The body stores memories that leave significant imprints on the brain, whether they are extreme expressions of joy or pain. A negative trigger brings up old low-potential thought patterns and causes you to feel overwhelmed and distressed in real time. It knocks you out of the present moment straight back into the past, in fear of reoccurrence here and now.

Triggers form the basis of your emotional calendar. These triggers may be seasons or anniversaries of an emotionally charged event such as the death of a loved one, a car accident, a severe illness, or other trauma. Once triggered by your emotional calendar, your subconscious causes the repetition of feelings and emotions. It can even cause similar events to occur.

Consciously, you may have no idea why you feel fatigued or depressed every spring. You may not understand why you have heart palpitations or accidents around this time. However, your subconscious knows why this happens. It sends emotional reminders as calendar notices. Once realized, you can mitigate distress by planning to be either actively distracted or consciously aware in acceptance on an anniversary.

Plotting out your own emotional calendar allows you to better navigate reoccurring imbalance.

Today, look at stressful recurring patterns in your life to see how they may be tied to your emotional calendar.

Expand your mind

Morning Thoughts

_____

_____

_____

_____

_____

_____

_____

Evening Summary and Insight Gained

_____

_____

_____

_____

_____

_____

_____

DAY 15

Be Aware of The Power of Your "I Am" Statements

At the root of mental balancing techniques is the act of valuing your self-worth. How you speak to yourself is a key indicator of self-esteem. Repeated self-talk shapes your identity. You orally express this through the words that you place after "I am."

What you put after "I am" has the building power to fuel your confidence and ambition. Conversely, it also has the destroying power to halt desire in its infancy and make you feel inadequate and anxious. Whether used to build or destroy, stating "I am" will resonate with more of the same energy in your life.

Used with power, the statement "I am" helps you discover unique abilities. This is not just using positive thinking; it is coloring future experiences with expectation based on knowing how powerful you are.

A simple statement such as "I am weak" can be replaced with "I am not yet strong enough," or even, "I am weak right now." This shifts you from lacking momentum to building momentum.

Subtle shifts yield the most on the scale of mental well-being.

Today, catch what you state after "I am." Make any adjustments needed to healthily shift the emotions that follow the statement.

Expand your mind

Morning Thoughts

_____

_____

_____

_____

_____

Evening Summary and Insight Gained

_____

_____

_____

_____

_____

_____

DAY 16
The Most Dangerous Battlefield Is an Unfocused Mind

Who is the enemy on your self-created battlefield? The enemy is your own doubt. Doubt that you can be good enough, happy enough, healthy enough, or abundant enough.

When we have doubts about our Creator-given abilities, uncertainty detracts from our ability to focus. Conversely, certainty is our greatest ally for centered focus.

In addition to doubt, there are distractions lurking everywhere. Technology, multi-tasking, and information overload are the primary culprits that exhaust your attentive energy. Look at how distractions are negatively affecting your life.

Another form of being emotionally unfocused is doing things that cause a conflict between the mind and heart. This internal conflict causes release of stress hormones—such as cortisol and adrenaline—that negatively affect blood pressure and heart rate. Consciously making a connection with your heart to ask what you should do and then visually syncing your heart and brain will get you back in focus.

Focus is a superpower we all have under our cape just waiting to be wielded. We just need to look at how and when we get distracted, doubt, or depart from our heart's intention, then bring our mind back to its present purpose.

Today, end the battle going on in your unfocused mind as it arises. Decide where you would like to focus. Then, allow your thoughts to take you there.

Expand your mind

Morning Thoughts

_____

_____

_____

_____

_____

_____

_____

Evening Summary and Insight Gained

_____

_____

_____

_____

_____

_____

DAY 17

Give Your Inner Critic a Hug

You are your worst critic. No one speaks to you more than the voice in your head. This voice, which often tells you that you are not good enough, strong enough, smart enough, rich enough, or imposing any other limited belief, is generated by your inner critic. Rather than measuring, comparing, and evaluating yourself, consider simply observing yourself and then accepting yourself. Free yourself from the burdensome thought that you must do or be more right now.

You will have to be vigilant. Negative self-thoughts can be so subtle you may not realize you are thinking them. Observation is the key to taming the critical narrative and to break through.

You can allow the critical voice its position without having a battle in your mind. Instead, gently direct your thoughts to a more balanced response, one that recognizes we are all works in progress.

Self-acceptance is allowing yourself to be wherever you are right now without judgement. Self-acceptance is an important mental balance tool because it allows you to surrender your ego's need to have everything occur in the manner and timing of your choice. It also quiets the inner critic long enough to hear a more subtle and primordial intelligence that tells you "Yes, you can," and how.

Today, observe the voice in your head's critical commentary and your emotional response to situations with as little judgement as possible. Just notice.

Expand your mind

Morning Thoughts

_____

_____

_____

_____

_____

_____

Evening Summary and Insight Gained

_____

_____

_____

_____

_____

_____

DAY 18

Resistance to What Is Causes Emotional Distress

Resistance comes from wanting something different from that which already is. Look at what you are resisting. Generally, it hinders you, as what you resist persists. What you resist grows even stronger as you give it more of your attention. Mental resistance is the source of suffering, not the situation itself.

Mental resistance is the degree to which an emotion prevents the flow of energy through it. Emotions such a fear, frustration, and rage have high resistance to the current flow of what is and cause energy blockages, which result in even more emotional distress.

When you try to pull away from emotions, inner conflict and fragmentation result. Trauma is pushed deeper into the body, rather than being allowed to heal and release. If you fight what is, you will lose. If you flee from what is, it will reappear in another form. Rather than resist unwanted experiences and emotions, practice observation and acceptance. No lower-potential emotion will overwhelm you if you move through it with awareness.

Observing emotions and situations with as little judgement as possible allows you to diminish resistance and break through. Each breakthrough during challenging times paves the way to emotional and spiritual growth. Each breakthrough confirms that you are stronger than you think. Life will always have ups and downs but going with the flow opens perspective that allows us to shift more rapidly to higher feeling emotions.

Today, when you feel the need to resist what the present moment places before you, observe, accept, and embrace the philosophy that life happens for you, not to you.

Expand your mind

Morning Thoughts

_____

_____

_____

_____

_____

_____

Evening Summary and Insight Gained

_____

_____

_____

_____

_____

_____

_____

DAY 19

Mental Imbalance Is Written All Over Your Face

Do not think you are stressed? Look in the mirror to see if you are frowning and notice if your jaw is clenched tightly. Both facial contractions induce more stress because they send the brain a message that something is wrong. This sets off the fight-or-flight mechanism, which prepares your body to take defensive action. A tense body keeps you in a perpetual state of fight or flight, which burdens the immune system and results in mind and body dis-ease. While the body is distracted by survival needs, your ability to be creative is diminished.

Consciously relax your forehead and/or loosen your jaw. This will help release the signal that sent the message to the brain to produce stress hormones.

A smile or laugh, however insincere, will also help, as it sends a positive message to the brain that the threat is gone. The brain does not know that you are faking it, and releases feel-good endorphins. So fake it until you can build up some resonance with the frequency of happiness.

Laughter is even more powerful than a smile as it engages more of the body. Laughter is a miracle drug that shifts everything. It triggers the release of endorphins, enhances feelings of general well-being, and reduces stress-hormone levels.

Laughter also allows you to free up space to think clearly. Best of all, it is free, healthy, fun, and contagious.

A sense of humor helps you stay balanced. When all else fails, find something funny and remember to laugh.

Today, when you feel a downward spiral in emotion attempting to tip the scale of your balance, jumpstart positive brain activity with a smile or laughter.

Expand your mind

Morning Thoughts

_____

_____

_____

_____

_____

_____

Evening Summary and Insight Gained

_____

_____

_____

_____

_____

_____

_____

DAY 20
Get Out of Your Mind

Are you constantly filling your mind with worries, projects, deadlines, or conflicts that result in endless mind chatter indicative of a mind full of thought? This chatter represents thoughts you have had many times before. You will not find anything new or self-expansive in this internal conversation.

Or are you out of your mind, mindful in observation, so that you can respond appropriately to stimulation and situations as they occur? This approach produces new, creative thought and action.

You are taught that being out of your mind is a negative. It is time to re-examine beliefs and teachings to begin to use the mind correctly to move out of patterns of thought and behavior that are no longer helpful.

Today, when you notice that your thoughts of what needs to be started or finished pull you away from the present moment, return to the present to see what you can do right now to resolve your concerns. The initial answer may be do nothing and simply be.

Expand your mind

Morning Thoughts

_____

_____

_____

_____

_____

_____

_____

Evening Summary and Insight Gained

_____

_____

_____

_____

_____

_____

_____

Balancing Act –
BREATH WORK

*T*he following breath therapy can help you get to a balanced state quickly.

Breathe in to the count of four, hold the breath to the count of two, and exhale to the count of eight. Extending the length of the exhalation triggers the parasympathetic nervous system by slowing down the heart rate and sending a message to the brain to go into relax and restore mode.

Breath work is an integral part of my day. At some point during more than twenty-five years of fervent multi-tasking at global corporations, I developed an attention deficit. It became hard for me to complete any one thing without starting another. Now, when I catch myself unnecessarily stopping one thing to start another, I use conscious breathing to slow down and return to focus. I also use conscious breathing to move through difficult tasks or situations to ward off worries of the future or recurrence of missteps from the past. I call on conscious breathing to transform my scattered thoughts to a wholeness that is centered in the present moment, which fosters productive clarity.

PHASE 3

SELF
ENCOUNTER

WE ARE BOTH A MASTERPIECE AND A WORK IN PROGRESS AT THE SAME TIME.

DAY 21

Invest in Yourself, as it Pays the Most Interest

Have you ever heard the expression, "Where your attention goes, energy flows?" If you want something to happen, get laser-focused on its occurrence. Invest your all into it. Engage all your emotions and senses through visualization. What does it look, feel, smell, sound, and even taste like?

Take time to learn as much as you can about your interests instead of spending time following the activities of the masses. If you paid the same amount of attention to your own life as most do the lives of celebrities and reality TV stars, you would be investing greater energy into your personal reality. Your thoughts would be your own, rather than reflections of someone else's thoughts.

You are exactly who you need to be. Instead of mimicking someone else, be your own star and shine the light of your unique self.

Investment in yourself always appreciates. The goal is not perfection. The goal is growth and expansion.

Today, notice where your external attention goes. Ask yourself if that attention could be better served if placed internally, on yourself.

Expand your mind

Morning Thoughts

_____

_____

_____

_____

_____

_____

_____

Evening Summary and Insight Gained

_____

_____

_____

_____

_____

_____

_____

DAY 22
Fuel Your Mind and It Will Fuel Your Body

The foods you eat are fuel — fuel for your body and your mind. Food is ultimately an energetic building block of happiness.

A true happy meal or snack consists of nourishing foods. Eating fast foods or highly processed foods leads to low energy and mental and physical illness.

On the metaphysical level, the thoughts you think fuel your emotions and drive experience. Just as there are junk foods, there are junk thoughts. These are low-potential thoughts that do as much harm to your mental being as junk food does to deplete the body.

Running on empty is not a viable option either. You need fuel to rev the engine of personal growth. You would not start off a long road trip with a quarter of a tank of gas and no expectation of stopping to get more. You know you would never reach your destination. Well, this is also true when it comes to fueling your mind and body to complete your heart's desire. Desire gets you to the quarter tank mark. High energy foods and thoughts top you off and create that extra reserve. Making conscious choices about where to focus your energy conserves fuel.

Similarly, you would not sit in your car complaining that your tank is on empty and you cannot go anywhere when you have money to buy gas. You would purchase gas and fill up. Our mental energy needs refueling in the same active manner.

A fuel reserve is needed for emergencies. This energy will carry you through when times are hard and you cannot get to a theoretical gas station to fill up.

Now, look in your pantry and refrigerator. Do you see foods that increase or decrease energy? When you need a mental boost, reach for fruit, vegetables, and good fats.

Today, consciously choose how to fuel your energy.

Expand your mind

Morning Thoughts

_____

_____

_____

_____

_____

_____

Evening Summary and Insight Gained

_____

_____

_____

_____

_____

_____

_____

DAY 23
Learn What Fuels Your Brain

What you eat impacts the efficiency with which neurotransmitters, the messengers of neurologic information from one cell to another in the body, do their work.

Feelings and emotions are produced by brain chemicals. The key neurotransmitters impacting feelings and emotions are:

Serotonin—called the happy drug because it is responsible for feelings of well-being and happiness. It is mainly found in the brain, the bowels, and blood platelets.

Dopamine—regulates emotional responses and is responsible for mood, attention, and learning.

GABA—creates the rhythmic, electrical impulses in the brain. It blocks, or slows, certain brain signals and decreases activity in the nervous system.

Norepinephrine—keeps us alert, awake and focused. It is released into the blood as a stress hormone when the brain perceives that a stressful event has occurred.

Eating foods from the list below keeps these neurotransmitters balanced by supplying:

- vitamin B12 and folic acid (poultry, seafood, leafy green vegetables, and citrus fruits)

- antioxidant phytochemicals (fruits, vegetables, beans and grains)

- selenium (broccoli, cabbage, spinach, seeds, i.e.: sunflower and flax)

- vitamin D (sun, mushrooms, fatty fish)

- dark chocolate (with low sugar content)

Take advantage of the season's bounty of fresh fruits and vegetables. Today, use food to boost your mood to generate high-potential thoughts that boost your emotional state.

Expand your mind

Morning Thoughts

_____

_____

_____

_____

_____

_____

_____

Evening Summary and Insight Gained

_____

_____

_____

_____

_____

_____

_____

DAY 24
Maintain Your Brain

Like physical fitness, you can practice mental fitness to avoid the below drivers of poor mental balance. Each symptom mentioned reduces needed energy to transmit strong, cohesive signals throughout the body.

Brain fog:

Cause: Dehydration (the brain is approximately 75 percent water)

Effect: Brain shrinkage that causes mild irritability or hallucinations

Impaired memory and learning:

Cause: Poor diet. A diet low in nutrients cannot nourish the brain causing poor information transfer across neural networks.

Effect: Fatigue and memory loss

Fatigue:

Cause: Lack of sleep. On average, the brain needs seven hours of sleep to produce enough serotonin, the body's natural happy drug.

Effect: Depression, moodiness

Fatigue:

Cause: Lack of exercise. Exercise pushes oxygen into the cells and stimulates endorphin production.

Effect: Sluggishness, foggy thinking

Today, notice when you feel fatigued, forgetful or dehydrated. Then, take account of what you can do to promote a reenergized state of being to be able to better enjoy your life.

Expand your mind

Morning Thoughts

_____

_____

_____

_____

_____

_____

Evening Summary and Insight Gained

_____

_____

_____

_____

_____

_____

DAY 25
Teach Your Brain New Tricks

Through ongoing developments in neuroplasticity—the ability of the brain to form new connections and pathways—and neurogenesis—the ability of the brain to grow new cells—scientists have abandoned the belief that the brain reaches a certain point in development and stays there.

The mind, via the brain, instructs the body to adapt to its needs. You benefit from moving this knowledge into action to encourage and stimulate your brain to form new connections and pathways, called neural networks, to adapt how your circuits are wired.

Through repetition, beneficial new connections can consciously replace those solidified by old habits, pain, fear, and/or trauma. These restructured neurological pathways send clear and healthy messages to the brain and body.

Practices that facilitate neuroplasticity include: exercise to increase blood flow, stimulation from learning new things, reducing stress, and mindfulness or paying attention in the moment.

When the mind shifts its focus from obstacles to possibilities, you begin to see alternatives that were always there.

Today, look for habits and self-patterns that may need to be upgraded to enhance well-being. Then, construct a plan to activate change in your brain.

Expand your mind

Morning Thoughts

_____

_____

_____

_____

_____

_____

Evening Summary and Insight Gained

_____

_____

_____

_____

_____

_____

_____

DAY 26
Tap into Your Second Brain

Your gut is the second brain. Some say it is the primary brain, as it was around before the complex brain evolved. The gut houses the largest collection of neurons (approximately 100 million) outside of the brain. It is important to sustain good gut health to ensure this network of neurons is efficiently sending and receiving information from your conscious body.

Gut feelings are quick, instinctual, and effortless. The information you receive in your gut is often expressed as butterflies (high-potential situations) or a sick feeling (low-potential situations). Trust your gut. Trust what feels right for you, and you will effortlessly tap into your power.

It is no coincidence that 95 percent of the well-being neurotransmitter serotonin resides in the gut. If you have problems with your gut and digestion, issues with nerves, anxiety, depression, or dis-ease (such as post-traumatic stress) often follow.

Today, observe when you have a gut feeling. See what happens when you either follow or ignore it.

Expand your mind

Morning Thoughts

_____

_____

_____

_____

_____

_____

Evening Summary and Insight Gained

_____

_____

_____

_____

_____

_____

_____

DAY 27

Energy Protection Is Essential to Well-being

You protect your mental energy in many ways, including:

- alone time,

- removal of things that clutter your space and energy,

- expressing how you feel,

- canceling commitments when feeling overwhelmed,

- changing your mind as you learn a higher truth,

- developing a sustaining personal mantra
  (mine is: Clarity, prosperity, and vitality are mine
  to share with all humanity),

- creating a home sanctuary where you can reflect,
  honor and meditate,

- grounding yourself in nature, and/or

- getting lost in soothing frequencies.

Opting out can be your first line of defense. Protect your energy with mental health days to restore balance and give you space for quiet reflection. Do this before it becomes an urgent need. All it takes is practice, intention, and knowing that mental well-being and balance are worth it.

Today, choose how you protect your energy from energy vampires (whether they be friends, family, the environment, or situations).

Expand your mind

Morning Thoughts

_____

_____

_____

_____

_____

_____

_____

Evening Summary and Insight Gained

_____

_____

_____

_____

_____

_____

_____

DAY 28
Go with the Rhythm of Your Personal Energy

Everything in the universe has its own ebb and flow. Do not try to do your life's equivalent of rocket science when you are in an ebb or rest stage. Wait for the flow.

When you feel out of tune, it is a sign that you are out of sync with your natural rhythm.

Pause for a reset. Just as spring follows winter, a season of flow will follow an ebb season. You will be reenergized. Similarly, when you are in a flow phase, take advantage of its abundant energy. It is there to be channeled and used creatively. Do not waste it through inaction or procrastination.

Honor your body temple and the rhythm of nature of which you are part. In fact, spend more time in natural environments to facilitate balance.

Today, think about the time of day or time of year when you feel that you are at your peak. Plan to do your creative and energy-intensive tasks at that time.

Expand your mind

Morning Thoughts

_____

_____

_____

_____

_____

_____

_____

Evening Summary and Insight Gained

_____

_____

_____

_____

_____

_____

_____

DAY 29

Use the Power of the Spoken Word

In a society where people are talking to each other less and less, it is necessary to reiterate how powerfully you can connect through your voice.

Energetic vibration is transmitted through the voice. You communicate more than just words. You transmit feelings and emotions, as well as memories. Griots pass on history and gurus transfer teachings in this way.

If you rarely speak with others, that sensory link is broken. You are missing out on unspoken information that is transmitted through tone and vibration. Without conversation, people tend to be less: less empathetic, less connected, less creative, and less fulfilled. Emojis and text messages cannot replace the vibrations that touch your mental, physical, and emotional bodies.

Spoken word has tremendous energy. Let us energize each other more.

Today, when you get ready to send a text, consider if speaking directly to someone will allow for enhanced communication.

Expand your mind

Morning Thoughts

_____

_____

_____

_____

_____

_____

Evening Summary and Insight Gained

_____

_____

_____

_____

_____

_____

_____

DAY 30
Be Equanimous in Troubled Times

You are an energetic being. Your life reflects your ability to harness the same energy that gives humans dominion over all things. You can harness this energy through your feelings.

Feelings, not things or actions, lead to well-being and happiness. Trying to change what is, is like moving around the chairs on the deck of the *Titanic*. It is too late. The ship is going down.

Think of those who successfully survived traumatic circumstances. They are the ones who did not give in to desolation. They focused on what could be done in the moment. They held fast to the thought that gave them the most balanced energy to allow them to move forward.

Developing the ability to be equanimous in troubled times comes from not being judgmental. It is judgement that causes suffering. Everything is seen through the eyes of perspective. Right or wrong is determined by the thinking mind and its perspective. When something has already occurred, why let it control you by continuing to recycle low-potential thoughts and action?

Today, if you find yourself becoming upset, see if you can shift to a neutral or equanimous position.

Expand your mind

Morning Thoughts

_____

_____

_____

_____

_____

_____

_____

Evening Summary and Insight Gained

_____

_____

_____

_____

_____

_____

_____

Balancing Act –
RAISE YOUR VIBRATION

The Inner Smile Meditation is a Taoist practice where you smile inwardly to major organs of our body. By giving the organs the attention of and energy of the smile, they are in turn energized. In turn, the organs send a message back to the brain to a more balanced frequency, and to the mind to enter a more expansive state. Here is a remarkably simple and effective modified version.

1. Sit comfortably with a straight spine. Close your eyes and feel connected to the earth through your feet. Imagine your tailbone extending into the earth, and the crown of your head into the sky.

2. Take a deep breath in, then exhale any tension. Take two more of these deep breaths. Begin with a soft smile from the lips and allow it to spread to the rest of your head. Revel in the joyous energy of a smile.

3. Let the smile spread down the entire body and then into your organs. Slowly move through five major organs with the smile: intestines, liver, spleen, kidney, lungs, and heart.

4. Notice how your body feels. If there are any areas of the body where you still feel distress, send an inner smile there until you feel the distress relieved.

5. Feel the aliveness of the energy field surrounding your body and rest in this heightened energy.

6. When you are ready to bring the meditation to a close, anchor this feeling of peace and contentment into your body by placing your hands over your heart. Take several deep breaths, then open your eyes.

This meditation is one of my favorites, as it can quickly take me from a low-potential mood to feeling energized and ready to attract vibrant life to me, instead of getting stuck in an emotion or defaulting to external energies.

PHASE 4

CONSCIOUS LIVING

ONCE YOU BEGIN DITCHING THOUGHTS THAT NO LONGER SERVE YOU, MORE ENERGIZED THOUGHTS WILL EMERGE THAT PROPEL YOU IN THE DIRECTION OF YOUR DESIRE.

DAY 31

The Only Thing Standing Between You and Your Goals Is the Story You Tell Yourself

Be mindful of the limiting stories you tell yourself. Self-stories impact how you feel, the chances you take, and the decisions you make. Through repetition, limiting self-stories put a ceiling on your reality.

We are all master storytellers. Your story reflects your perception of life. Through perception, you see people and events through the lenses of fear, desire, and programming rather than how they really are.

An example of a limiting story is, "I am never going to ace this assignment; it is just too hard."

When you face a limiting story like this, ask yourself:

- What is my level of investment in this story?

- Is it true today?

- How could it be told to yield a better outcome?

- What is the more purposeful version of my story?

A limiting story loses more power every time you question it. Shifting the story until it becomes an uplifting one leads to a more conducive life experience.

Transformed to yield a better outcome, the above limiting story could sound like this:

"I do not know if I can ace this test, but I can seek help to give it my best shot."

If you wish to continually grow, pursue your dreams, accomplish goals, and feel complete, the uplifting stories you tell yourself (and others) must outnumber the limiting ones.

Today, watch for self-limiting narratives, then see how you might reshape them into uplifting narratives.

Expand your mind

Morning Thoughts

_____

_____

_____

_____

_____

_____

_____

Evening Summary and Insight Gained

_____

_____

_____

_____

_____

_____

_____

DAY 32
Reset Your Point of Attraction

You have the power to make healthy choices, not just for the body but for the mind also. Intentionally holding a focused mind that is not stressed, anxious or fearful is the best thing you can do for yourself. It is the foundation of self-love, self-care, and, ultimately, a balanced life.

Train your mind. Focus on the thoughts that get you to well-being. Thoughts attract like things and ripple more of the same energy into your world. It is divine law that like attracts like (versus the opposites-attract model that you may have been taught).

Everything in your life experience is an outcome of probability. Your thoughts attract the probability that matches the frequency of an emotion or feeling. This becomes your point of attraction. That is why you must feel your way to balanced energy before just doing something.

Hosting a majority of balanced thoughts leads to a happier experience. As a simple example, if someone steps on your toe when you are feeling happy, your response is different from what it is if the same situation happens while you were angry. In the first situation, you may have compassion. In the second, you may feel irritation.

As you get older, you accumulate life's disappointments. If disappointment has been the majority of your experience or your energy-attraction point, then life may not be much fun. Training your mind to host helpful core thoughts or underlying beliefs about self, other people and the world you live in will help you reset your point of attraction.

Today, when your energy becomes imbalanced practice resetting your attraction point by raising your vibrational frequency.

Expand your mind

Morning Thoughts

_____

_____

_____

_____

_____

_____

_____

Evening Summary and Insight Gained

_____

_____

_____

_____

_____

_____

_____

DAY 33
Healing Emotional Wounds Helps You Be More Present in Life

Emotional wounds are often more difficult to heal than physical wounds. This is because deep hurt or pain lies beneath the surface, often unrealized or unacknowledged. They are reopened by events, people, or places that cause us to replay the story of mistreatment, abandonment, or victimization. We all have these unhealed places within us. It is part of being human. Emotional wounds will always float to the surface to be healed because your mind, body, and spirit automatically seek a steady state of balance.

Unhealed wounds act to filter your view of the present moment through the experience of past pain. You will miss the full potential of a situation because your unbalanced mind is looking to protect you from the same expected threats. This action filters out new possibilities.

When you examine the cycle of these triggers and reactions to pain, you can uncover the underlying stories and begin to heal the wounds. This is much more advantageous than ripping off your emotional scabs during knee-jerk reactions and experiencing more pain. You can heal and move forward at the same time. The process of healing promotes stabilized calm, which improves your quality of life. Awareness is the first step. Unlearning is the next. Patience and gentleness are the salve. Time will facilitate the rest.

Today, think about what emotional wounds you have that still require healing. Treat yourself with loving care as you begin to validate yourself and use time to heal your emotional wounds.

Expand your mind

Morning Thoughts

_____

_____

_____

_____

_____

_____

_____

Evening Summary and Insight Gained

_____

_____

_____

_____

_____

_____

_____

DAY 34

Mental Balance Is Not Dependent Upon Happiness

Let us first clear up some myths on happiness. Happiness is not:

1. A destination. It is what happens by default on life's journey when you are not resisting what is before you. Being unhappy with a current situation does not preclude being happy in life.

2. One size fit all. There is no perfect body, weight, style, job, bank account, home, car, or relationship that is right for all of us. We all have individual backgrounds, preferences, and cultural experiences.

3. Perfection. You can get stuck or feel that you are not enough when you strive for perfection. Satisfaction with your current best gives you way more bang for your buck.

4. A formula derived from accumulating material possessions. The perceived right partner, clothes, shoes, house, car, and so on will never lead to mental balance.

No matter how joyful or horrendous a situation, good mental balance fosters the ability to respond appropriately.

Today, practice maintaining mental balance even when the situation before you causes you to feel unhappy.

Expand your mind

Morning Thoughts

_____

_____

_____

_____

_____

_____

Evening Summary and Insight Gained

_____

_____

_____

_____

_____

_____

_____

DAY 35
Love Promotes Emotional and Physical Well-Being

Love is as critical to a balanced life as food or water. Yet what society portrays as romantic love through media is not true love. Therein lies disillusionment that can lead to emotional imbalance, jealousy, and anger. These emotions can lead to rage and depression. When you lose in romantic love, you may feel betrayed and inadequate.

But love is never lost. It continues in relationships all around us—with the Creator, nature, animals, children, friends and family, and most importantly, with ourselves. Self-love is defined as *"regard for one's own happiness or advantage"*. Self-love is dynamic; it grows the more you practice appreciating your individual uniqueness.

Practicing relationship building includes self-love, overcoming differences, developing empathy for others, enhancing communication skills, and letting go when core differences take too much of an emotional toll. These are all examples of love in practice.

We all need loving support networks—family, friends, and colleagues—who help us through stressful situations. We need someone to bounce thoughts off and to reflect how we are showing up in the world. Studies have shown that socially isolated people are less able to deal with stressful situations. The immune system responds to social isolation by releasing stress hormones and causing inflammation. Depression, high anxiety, poor sleep quality, and cognitive decline can all result from social isolation. Forced isolation by peers—a form of bullying—has the same effect.

Today, look at your love relationships (with self, friends, family, and significant others) to see where you place conditions on the relationship that detract from your emotional and physical well-being.

Expand your mind

Morning Thoughts

_____

_____

_____

_____

_____

_____

Evening Summary and Insight Gained

_____

_____

_____

_____

_____

_____

DAY 36
View "Failure" as a Dry Run

Everyone fails. Lack of failure means you have never tried anything new. Yet fear of failure is the number-one reason most people do not go after their desires. When you let others define failure for you and worry about what they will think, failure is associated with embarrassment, disappointment, and setbacks.

Failure redefined can be viewed as a steppingstone. You learned what did not work, now you can move forward better informed. It is helpful to shift perspective from going back to the drawing board in defeat to moving forward to the drawing board with enhanced knowledge.

Instead of trying to run away from emotions associated with failure, such as anxiety, fear, and shame, allow yourself to experience them, let out any frustration, then shift to expectation of a better outcome. Remember, every emotion is an indicator. Fear warns you to prepare for immediate action. Anxiety says get ready to take on something you do not yet know how to deal with. Shame, one of the lowest frequency emotions, is a negative self-evaluation. Shame is associated with deep feelings of powerlessness and worthlessness when societal norms are violated. Shame never reflects the truth of who you are.

Life is full of learning opportunities, even if they do not feel like opportunities when experienced.

Today, find opportunities to shift your perspective of failure when things do not go the way you plan.

Expand your mind

Morning Thoughts

_____

_____

_____

_____

_____

_____

Evening Summary and Insight Gained

_____

_____

_____

_____

_____

_____

_____

DAY 37

Forgiveness Is for You

Forgiveness is a gift of self-love. It is a process of transmuting resentful energy into neutrality. Forgiveness graduates you from being stuck in the past to viewing people and situations with the present moment in mind to release perspectives that no longer serve you.

Forgiveness is not forgetting, condoning or excusing; rather it is moving forward for your own energetic liberation. While you cannot undo the perceived transgression, forgiveness paves a path to gently self-correct your perspective and find your way to balanced emotions so that the future is not impacted by the past.

Forgiveness does not require you to feel good about the other person. It provides relief through dropping the emotionally heavy baggage of deeply held low-potential emotions such as resentment, anger, betrayal, fear, or abandonment.

In the game of life, forgiveness trumps all mental suffering. Knowing this empowers you to recognize the emotional pain you suffered without letting that pain define you, enabling you to heal and move forward with a joyful and balanced heart.

Forgiveness becomes easier when you can recognize what past transgression someone plays out in the current time rubs salt into an already-open emotional wound. Can that original emotional wound now be closed with your acknowledgement that forgiveness is for you?

Today, express compassion for yourself by seeing where you can realize the value of forgiveness.

Expand your mind

Morning Thoughts

_____

_____

_____

_____

_____

_____

Evening Summary and Insight Gained

_____

_____

_____

_____

_____

_____

_____

DAY 38
Your Unique Self Is a Gift to the World

There is good stress (eustress) and bad stress (distress). Helpful stress occurs when you are excited without feeling threatened or fearful. It is vital to personal growth. Bad stress occurs when stressful energy is not channeled toward a solution and the fight-or-flight mechanism is left on long past the event that triggered it.

In today's society, most bad stress is caused by trying to be whom are what you are not. When you conform to the opinions of others rather than voicing your own opinion or go with the flow rather than setting your own agenda, mental distress results.

The social pressure to conform to the norm is tremendous, so it can be hard to pave your unique path in life through liberation from beliefs that you have been force-fed. Start by recognizing your strong qualities and finding ways to express them.

Be creative.

Help others.

Keep showing up with your uniqueness. This is the area where you will excel. It is also the unique piece that only you can contribute to complete the world puzzle.

Do not let fear hold you back. Fear comes from who you are not, not who you are now. Embracing your uniqueness means releasing fearful perceptions of self in order to grow.

Honor your unique path. It takes courage to walk it. Be bold.

Today, just be yourself. Observe when you fall out of alignment with your uniqueness, then energetically step back in. Notice how great it feels.

Expand your mind

Morning Thoughts

_____

_____

_____

_____

_____

_____

_____

Evening Summary and Insight Gained

_____

_____

_____

_____

_____

_____

_____

DAY 39

Gift Yourself with Mental Balance

Feelings of inadequacy and lack directly contribute to emotional imbalance and mental distress. Remember to appreciate yourself and give thanks for all that you have.

The truth is you do not need things. You need a balanced mind. A mind free from despair and fear can navigate physical and emotional barriers to obtain not only what you need but also what you desire.

You can always tap into balance. It is likely just buried under your beliefs and attachments, waiting to be uncovered. Know that distressing beliefs do not hold real power over you, because you can always shift them.

Reading, viewing, or listening to uplifting information, meditating, exercising, getting sufficient sleep and water, eating nutritious foods, and engaging in talk therapy can all help you change your state of being to a mind at ease or balance.

These actions all build up your mental immunity, ensuring that you do not absorb environmental distress or become stuck in a personal pattern of despair. With a strong mental immune system, your mind is free to find creative solutions.

Today, when external events do not live up to your expectations, see what beliefs are prohibiting you from experiencing balance. Then, re-center and gift yourself with a balanced being—a gift that keeps on giving.

Expand your mind

Morning Thoughts

_____

_____

_____

_____

_____

_____

_____

Evening Summary and Insight Gained

_____

_____

_____

_____

_____

_____

DAY 40
It Is Your Responsibility to Stay Grounded

It takes strength to pull yourself out of a dark place. The world can wear you down with its constant changes and challenges, yet most of your personal growth comes from intense experiences and successfully moving through turbulent emotions. What practices or traditions do you have to keep you balanced and on track?

Use mental balance tools to tap into good vibrations: meditation, dance, art, musical instruments (including the voice), talk therapy, healing herbs, being in nature, singing bowls, moving meditation (yoga, tai chi, etc.), and aromatherapy. These techniques have stood the test of time because they are excellent sources of high-potential energy.

They all soothe the savage beast or dissonance within to allow you to resonate with your best self. It is essential that you build your personal balance toolkit.

Self-balance also includes finding your tribe of like-minded companions who help keep you emotionally and spiritually lifted.

Trust that your choices are supported by the same Source Energy that creates worlds. You hold that much power. Harness it through staying grounded.

Today, if you feel your energy level decreasing, have some fun with one of these grounding tools. See how it elevates your spirit.

Expand your mind

Morning Thoughts

_____

_____

_____

_____

_____

_____

Evening Summary and Insight Gained

_____

_____

_____

_____

_____

_____

_____

Balancing Act –
TAP INTO YOUR HIGHER SELF

*T*he object of this balancing act is to allow your mind, body, and spirit to become one to experience a more authentic and grounded you—one deeper than what is experienced at the thought level. From this space, you can move in harmony with the flow of life, receive guidance from your higher self, and tap into collective consciousness.

For this exercise, we are using the sound frequency of 432 Hertz (Hz) as it aligns with emotional healing and clarity. This is the frequency of peace, love, and general well-being. It is also the frequency of the heartbeat of the planet Earth. You can find 432 Hz music and frequencies on YouTube. Relax into some classical music at 432 Hz, or use your instinct to see which selections resonate with you. Trust yourself to select wisely.

1. Sit comfortably with a straight spine. Close your eyes and feel connected to the earth through your feet. Imagine your tailbone extending into the earth, and the crown of your head into the sky.

2. Take a deep breath in, then exhale any tension. Take two more of these deep breaths.

3. As you listen, feel your body aligning to this frequency. Visualize emotional blockages being released and relax into a feeling of being connected with All That Is.

4. Once done, take a few centering deep breaths before opening your eyes to enter your space re-energized. Know that no matter how fleeting the feeling may be, a shift to a higher vibration and calmer self is taking place. I also have frequencies playing in the background as I move throughout the day. For me, part of the beauty after doing this exercise is that I no longer feel as though an intangible something is missing. I experience wholeness.

In Closing

"The greatest accomplishment in the world is knowing how to align with oneself."

–Raiysa Nazaire

Strong mental balance is much more than the absence of mental illness. It allows for mental resilience that makes you focused, flexible, and productive no matter what is going on in your environment. It allows you to return to the center of your being whenever you become misaligned to enjoy a fruitful life experience.

In summary, I leave you with seven major keys to balanced energy and mental well-being.

1. Examine your thoughts. They are not created equally.

2. Use your emotions as directional indicators, not dictators.

3. Fuel your brain.

4. Set time for a regular practice to bring you back to balance, such as reflection and meditation.

5. Connect with your uniqueness and continue to learn in order to improve.

6. Make time for relaxation and play.

7. Your personal experience of balance is unique. Be your authentic self.

Only you can set the self-focus that gives you control of your response to life experience. In the juggling act of life, it is okay to drop a ball. Dropped balls represent experience, and experience is the best teacher of self-mastery. Juggling masterfully represents being in the present moment. The present moment is where life's magic happens.

Mental well-being or balance is your natural set point. When you use this truth as an anchor, you create a stable foundation for yourself that can carry you through the ebb and flow of life. Mental balance strengthens you. It allows a shift with a sense of purpose to build a stronger, happier, and more focused version of yourself. Even if you do not see evidence of this change at first, your energy is shifting. Embrace it!

Balance is eternally dynamic because change is inevitable. The wobble that you experience while surfing for emotional balance is a teacher. It lets you know how far you are from being centered. While the wobble never disappears, it does become more imperceptible with practice.

The unalome symbol used throughout the book is a symbol of life being a journey towards balance in a world where you are exploring duality. You go through contrasting ups and downs—the good and the bad—as part of a learning process that fosters higher and higher levels of consciousness awareness, if you allow it.

You always have the ability to move through thoughts and emotions to find balance in any experience. Trust what feels right for you.

Happy balancing!

Call to Action!

Thank you for reading my book!

As you emerge from your virtual Noah's ark after forty days of well-being concepts and self-exploration, you are now equipped with the fortitude to be a mental revolutionary who guides the way into a new era of balanced living. What makes this revolutionary?

1. You have been called to question what you think you know, including releasing limiting preconceived notions of what mental health and balance are.

2. You are being asked to reassess the purpose of life as mental expansion and evolution versus simply physical growth and accumulation of resources.

3. You took the time to align your mental and physical being to allow a wholeness of self that fosters living your unique purpose.

4. Your change creates a ripple effect that motivates others to change. Once others see the change in you, they will want to know what caused it. Share your experience, as experience is the best teacher.

Balance—like life—is a journey, not a destination. Keep moving forward.

I love to receive feedback. I need your input to make the next version of this book and my future books better. Please leave me a helpful review on Amazon, letting me know what you thought of the book. If you have not already downloaded the free companion e-book, *Your Balance Toolkit*, to structure your personal balance building and maintenance plan, please do so now at https://designrr.page/?id=93884&token=2501024811&type=FP/.

Thank you so much!

−Raiysa Nazaire

About the Author

Raiysa Darlene Nazaire has been a seeker (and sharer) of truth her entire life. Her own personal truth was experienced through a myriad of sources, including Islam and Sufism, A Course in Miracles, Kabbalah, New Thought and Unity Consciousness, Mind Management, Secret Energy, and Intuitive Astrology. Raiysa used this unique combination of consciousness to develop her personal modality of teaching well-being through the intersection of psychology and spirituality.

Balance Is a Juggling Act being her second self-help book on mental well-being and exemplifies this intersection. Her first work, *Leaping Over the Hurdles of Life: A Tiger's Journey,* depicts her son's poignant struggle with mental distress and shares mental well-being maintenance tips and awareness.

While writing *Leaping Over the Hurdles of Life,* Raiysa realized how uneducated we are as a global community about true mental health, and she embarked on becoming a mental-health advocate and life coach. *Balance Is a Juggling Act* is the product of Raiysa's studies and personal experience of managing (and mismanaging) both everyday life's normal and traumatic stressors, using spiritual concepts as a springboard for mental expansion.

Raiysa is a certified life coach, podcast host, entrepreneur, and CEO of two not-for-profits organizations, Young Tigers Foundation for suicide awareness and prevention and Sisters in Spirit Inc., which helps women infuse harmony into their daily living. She is a board member of Chess & Community, whose mission is to teach youth to "think before you move," and the Guap Foundation, a cryptocurrency fostering economic empowerment in black and brown communities. Raiysa is a Project Management Professional (PMP) with a master's degree in project management. She thrives on sharing knowledge and information that empowers others to be their absolute best.

Raiysa can be contacted via

raiysatheauthor.com

or

http://www.raiysanazaire.com